Everton

Mike Wilson

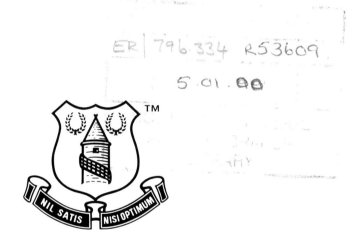

NIL SATIS NISI OPTIMUM

Published in association with The Basic Skills Agency

Hodder & Stoughton

A MEMBER OF THE HODDER HEADLINE GROUP

Acknowledgements

Photos: pp. iv, 8, 12, 24 and 28 © Allsport, pp. 6 and 16 © Popperfoto, p. 20 © Action-Plus.
Cover photo: © Allsport.

The publishers would like to thank Everton FC and their sponsors for their kind assistance in producing this book.

OFFICIAL CLUB SPONSOR

OFFICIAL KIT SPONSOR

Orders: please contact Bookpoint Ltd, 39 Milton Park, Abingdon, Oxon OX14 4TD. Telephone: (44) 01235 400414, Fax: (44) 01235 400454. Lines are open from 9.00–6.00, Monday to Saturday, with a 24 hour message answering service. Email address: orders@bookpoint.co.uk

British Library Cataloguing in Publication Data
A catalogue record for this title is available from The British Library

ISBN 0 340 71166 3

First published 1998
Impression number 10 9 8 7 6 5 4 3 2 1
Year 2003 2002 2001 2000 1999 1998

Typeset by Fakenham Photosetting Ltd, Fakenham, Norfolk
Printed in Great Britain for Hodder & Stoughton Educational, a division of Hodder Headline Plc, 338 Euston Road, London NW1 3BH by Page Bros Ltd, Norfolk.

Contents

Goodison Park.

All football teams
have a nick-name.
Ours is the 'Toffee Men'.

The name comes from a sweet shop.
It is called Mother's Toffee Shop.
The shop was near our ground,
Goodison Park.
They sold toffee to the fans
when there was a match on.

We are still called the Toffees,
or the Toffee Men.

We are Everton FC,
the pride of Merseyside!

1 Early Days

Everton Football Club
began life in 1878.

It began as a sports club.
The club was part of St. Domingo's Church.
St. Domingo's was in Everton.
Everton is a part of the city of Liverpool.

At St. Domingo's, they played sport.
They played cricket in the summer.
They played football in the winter.
The football team
was called the St. Domingo Football Club.

In the early days,
we had our best ever win:
11–2 against Derby County!

Our ground is Goodison Park.
We have not always played there.

We have played at Stanley Park,
Priory Road and Anfield Road.

We moved to Goodison in 1892.
We have been there over a hundred years.

Back then,
Goodison was the best ground in England.
The FA Cup Final
was played there in 1894.

This was long before the Cup Final
moved to Wembley.

Everton moved to Goodison in 1892,
but some of the players
stayed at Anfield.

That was how Liverpool FC started.
They were born out of Everton FC!

The two teams,
Everton and Liverpool,
became big rivals.
And we've been rivals ever since.

The first time we played Liverpool,
at Goodison Park, in 1894,
we won 3–0.

When they played us at Anfield,
it was 2–2.

First blood to the Toffee Men!

We were a good team
in the early days.
We got to the FA Cup Final
in 1893 and 1897.
But we lost both games.

Then in 1906 we won the FA Cup.
We beat Newcastle 1–0.

In 1907 we were in the Final again.
But we lost to Sheffield Wednesday.

Four finals.
Only one win.
Not a good track record!

Still, we showed
we could win the League as well:
Once in 1890–91.
Once in 1914–15.

2 Between the Wars

Between the wars,
the Toffees' playing was very up and down.

We won the League in 1927–28.
But in 1929–30,
we went down to the Second Division!

(This was before the days
of the Premier League.
The top division was called
League Division One.)

The next year the Toffees went back up.
Back to the top division.
The very next season, 1931–32,
we won the League again!

In 1933 Everton played for the Cup.
It was the first ever Wembley Final.
We beat Manchester City 3–0.

Everton with the 1933 FA Cup.

3 Goal Scorers

William 'Dixie' Dean helped
Everton to do so well.

He was Everton's centre forward.
He was world class.
He was good with his head.
And he could score
with both his feet.

He was our top goal scorer.
He was the best ever.

In the 1927–28 season,
he scored 60 goals.
And nobody has ever beaten
that record.

Not Alan Shearer.
Not George Best.
Not Cantona.

Not even Duncan Ferguson,
one of our stars today.

The great Dixie Dean.

When Dixie Dean was too old to play,
a young man took his place.
He was called Tommy Lawton.

In 1938–39,
Tommy Lawton was only 19.
But he was top scorer that season.
He got 34 goals.

Everton helped themselves
to another League Championship!

Then World War Two began.
There was no football until 1946.

By then,
Tommy Lawton had moved to Chelsea.

His career went downhill
when he left Everton.
He was never that good again.

But when Tommy Lawton left,
Everton went downhill as well.
We didn't win anything
for nearly 20 years!

4 The School of Science

It was 1963
before the Toffees won anything else.

In the 1962–63 season,
we won the League.
We didn't lose a single match
at home all season.

Then, in 1966,
the year of England's World Cup win,
Everton won the FA Cup Final.
We beat Sheffield Wednesday (again) 3–2.

But the Toffees made it hard
for themselves.
We were 2–0 down,
but we still came back to win
with three late goals!

We should have gone into Europe
in 1968.
But Liverpool were in the same competition.
The rules said
only one team from each town.
So Liverpool went into Europe,
and we stayed at home.

No wonder we don't like Liverpool FC!

The Everton team of 1970
was nick-named 'The School of Science'.
This was because
they played such good football.

The Toffees won the League that season.
That was League title number seven.

The star players were
World Cup hero Alan Ball,
Colin Harvey, Howard Kendall
and Joe Royle.
The last three were also top
Everton managers.

Everton v Liverpool: the great rivals.

But the Toffees didn't win everything.

In 1971, we lost to Liverpool
in the FA Cup semi-final.
The same thing happened in 1977.

It's never very nice losing to Liverpool.
But in an FA Cup semi-final
it's really bad news.

In 1977,
we also lost in the League Cup Final.
We lost 3–2 to Aston Villa.

So near and yet so far!

5 Glory Days

Howard Kendall became
Everton manager in 1981.
He made a slow start.

By 1984, we had not won anything.
Then we lost to Liverpool (again!)
in the League Cup Final.

Some fans wanted Howard
to get the sack.
But in the same year,
we won the FA Cup.
Andy Gray
was on the score sheet.

That was the start
of Everton's glory days.

1984–85 started well.
We beat Liverpool
in the Charity Shield.

Then we won the League
(title number eight).
We made it to the FA Cup Final,
but lost 1–0 to Manchester United.

Never mind.

There was still
the European Cup Winners' Cup Final.
We beat Rapid Vienna 3–1.
And we made it look so easy!
Our one and only European trophy.

It was the best Everton team ever.
We were all set for the next season.
We could conquer Europe again.

But it was not to be.

Everton with the 1985 European Cup Winners' Cup.

Way back in 1892,
Everton and Liverpool FC split.
We became two clubs.
Since then we have been big rivals.

Ninety years later, in the 1980s,
we were still rivals.

We had a brilliant team.
We had brilliant players,
like Andy Gray, Peter Reid,
Neville Southall and Gary Lineker.

But it was Liverpool
who won all the big matches.

In 1986,
they beat us in the FA Cup Final.
And they won the League that year too.
We were second – just two points behind!

In the FA Cup Final, the score was 3–1.
Our star striker, Gary Lineker,
had put us in the lead
with the best goal of the match.

(Everton had got to the final
three years in a row.)

Still, next year we got our revenge!
Everton won the League in 1987.
We were nine points ahead of Liverpool.

Gary Lineker, our top scorer,
had left and gone to Spain.
But we still won the League without him.

In all,
manager Howard Kendall
used 23 players to get us there.
So it really was a team effort!

Then Howard Kendall followed Lineker,
and took a job in Spain.
Colin Harvey took over the team.

Gary Lineker playing for Everton.

We won the Charity Shield in 1987.
But after that,
we had a run of bad luck.

We made it to the FA Cup Final in 1989
– but Liverpool beat us!

In 1984, our manager, Colin Harvey, left.
Howard Kendall came back to Everton
for a year as manager.
And then we signed another manager,
Mike Walker, from Norwich.

But Everton kept on getting
nearer the danger zone.

The club had money troubles at that time.
Star players –
like Peter Beardsley, and Peter Beagrie –
had to be sold and were not replaced.

Then we beat Wimbledon 3–2
in the last match of the season.
It was just enough
to keep us in the new Premier League.

6 The Royle Years

After years in the shadows,
it was time for something good to happen
to Everton Football Club.

That something was Joe Royle.

He was Everton's star striker in the 1970s.
He scored 119 goals in 275 games
for the Toffees.
He came back to Goodison
in November 1994.
This time as star manager.

His first match in charge was a big one.
It was against Liverpool.

But Joe and the team were up to it:
we won 2–0.

7 Big Dunc

Joe Royle had a new striker.
He put a lot of faith in him.
His name was Duncan Ferguson.
He was a big striker.
Just as Joe had been.

The fans couldn't wait
for Big Dunc to settle in at Goodison.
He was such a great player.

Duncan Ferguson celebrates another goal.

For Everton fans,
Big Dunc could do no wrong.
He scored in a great 2–0 win against Liverpool.

In May 1995 we played Manchester United.
Duncan Ferguson came on as a substitute.
It was our 5th FA Cup win.

Big Dunc was not 100% fit.
He didn't score.
But he did his bit
in a famous victory.

It was Paul Rideout who scored for us
after 30 minutes.

After that,
Manchester United threw everything at us.
But we hung on to that narrow lead,
and beat them 1–0.

Our captain, Dave Watson,
was Man of the Match.
But the real hero that day
was Neville Southall.

At 36, he made some brilliant saves.
He kept us one goal up,
right to the final whistle.

At long last, the glory days were back!
Joe Royle had put the Toffees
back where we belong.

But it was not to last.

In 1995–96,
we finished 6th in the League.
No prizes there.

And in 1996–97,
we sank fast.
Right to the bottom of the table.
In 13 matches, we won only 2.

In Cup matches, we lost to giant killers:
Bradford in the FA Cup;
York in the Coca Cola Cup.

In January 1997
FA Cup Final hero Neville Southall
was dropped.
Without him, the Toffees lost 4–1
to Newcastle.

When Joe Royle took the manager's job,
he said it was a dream come true.
He said:

'I'd like to think
I'll be here as long as I live!'

Two years later,
the dream had become a bit of a nightmare.

Enough was enough.
Joe Royle left Everton
in March 1997.

And the search
for the Toffees' new manager began.